Joshua 1-9

"God's Plan For Spiritual Victory"

A Bible-Based Study
For Individuals And Groups
Complete With Leader's Guide

Lamplighters International
Eden Prairie, Minnesota, USA 55344
www.LamplightersUSA.org

Third printing – October, 2003
Lamplighters International
Eden Prairie, Minnesota USA 55344

Lamplighters International is a Christian ministry that publishes Christ-centered discipleship and teaching resources.

For additional information about the Lamplighters ministry resources contact:
Lamplighters International P. O. Box 44725, Eden Prairie, Minnesota USA 55344 or visit our website at www.LamplightersUSA.org.

ISBN # 1-931372-00-4.
Order # Jo1-NK-SS

Contents

How To Use This Manual

What is Lamplighters?

Lamplighters is a Christ-centered ministry that is designed to increase your understanding of God's Word and equip you to serve Him more effectively. The ministry consists of a series of teaching and discipleship resources for churches, small groups and individuals, leadership training materials and student resources.

This Lamplighters Self-Study can be used individually as a personal devotional guide or as a study guide for a small group Bible study. It can also be used as a student booklet for an adult Bible class. Each lesson within this study is a self-contained unit and an integral part of the entire Lamplighters discipleship ministry.

This Lamplighters study is comprised of six or twelve individual lessons, depending on the format you choose. When you have completed the entire study you will have a much greater understanding of a significant portion of God's Word. You will also have learned several new truths that you can apply to your life.

How to study a Lamplighters lesson.

A Lamplighters study begins with prayer, your Bible, the weekly lesson, and a sincere desire to learn more about God's Word. The questions are presented in a progressive sequence as you work through the study material. You should not use biblical commentaries and other biblical reference books until you have completed your weekly lesson and met with your weekly group. When you approach the Bible study in this way, you will have the opportunity to discover valuable personal insights from the Word of God.

First, find a quiet place to complete your weekly lesson. You will need approximately twenty to thirty minutes to complete each lesson (Part "A" or "B". If you are new to Lamplighters, plan to spend more time on the first few lessons. Your weekly personal study time will decrease as you become familiar with the format. Soon you will look forward to discovering important life principles in the coming lessons.

Some people complete their weekly lesson at one time but others have found it beneficial to complete the studies on two different occasions. If you approach your study time in this way you will be able to reflect more fully upon difficult biblical passages. For those meeting as part of a study group or a Sunday School class, the pastor or teacher will be available to help you find the answers to those difficult questions. Many people have found it helpful to begin their study early in the week so that they have enough time to meditate on the questions that require careful consideration.

Your answers should be written in your own words in the space provided on the weekly studies with appropriate verse references unless the question calls for a personal opinion. The answers to the questions will be found in the Scripture references at the end of the questions or in the passages listed at the beginning of each study.

How to use this study guide.

The Lamplighters discipleship materials are designed for a variety of ministry applications. They have been used successfully in the following settings.

Self-study - Read the passage that is listed at the beginning of the weekly lesson. Seek to gain as much understanding from the Text as possible. Answer the questions in the space provided, using complete sentences if the space allows. Complete the entire lesson without looking at the Leader's Guide in the back of the book. Discipline yourself to answer all the questions so that you gain the maximum benefit from the lesson. When you have completed the lesson, read the corresponding portion of the Leader's Guide to gain greater understanding of the passage you have just studied.

One-on-one discipleship - Complete the entire lesson without referring to the Leader's Guide. If you are leading the one-on-one discipleship time meeting, become familiar with the Leader's Guide answers before you meet with the person you are discipling. Plan to meet for approximately one hour to discuss the lesson. Do not look at the Leader's Guide until you have met with the person who is leading the meeting.

Small Group discipleship - The members of the discipleship group should complete their weekly lessons without referring to the Leader's Guide. The Group Leader should complete the lesson before he becomes thoroughly familiar with the Leader's Guide answers. A comprehensive ministry manual has been prepared for church leaders to help them in leading small groups effectively and how to implement the Lamplighters discipleship ministry into their church ministries.

Class teaching (Adult or Senior High Sunday School Classes) - The pastor or teacher should complete the entire lesson before class, review the Leader's Guide answers, and prayerfully consider how to present the lesson. The class members should complete their weekly lessons in advance so that they can bring their thoughtful insights and questions to the class discussion time. The Teacher's Edition makes an excellent companion to this format and allows the teacher to design specific lessons appropriate in length and knowledge level for the students. Contact Lamplighters or visit our website for more information about how to combine these two products.

"*Do you think*" Questions

Each weekly study has a few "*do you think*" questions. These questions ask you to make personal applications from the Biblical truths you are learning. Make a special effort to answer these questions because they are designed to help you apply God's Word to your life. In the first lesson the *"do you think"* questions are placed in italic print for easy identification. If you are part of a Sunday School class or a small group Bible Study, your insightful answers to these questions could be a great source of spiritual encouragement to others.

Personal Questions

Occasionally you will be asked to respond to personal questions that you should do your best to answer. If you are part of a study group, you will not be asked to share any personal information about yourself. However, be sure to answer these questions for your own benefit because they will help you compare your present level of spiritual maturity to the Biblical principles presented in the lesson.

A Final Word

Throughout this study the masculine pronouns are often used in the generic sense to avoid awkward sentence construction. When the pronouns "he", "him", "his" are used to refer to the Trinity (God the father, Jesus Christ and the Holy Spirit), they always refer to the masculine gender.

This *Lamplighters* study is presented after many hours of careful preparation. It is our prayer that it will help you *"... grow in grace and in the knowledge of our Lord and Savior Jesus Christ. To Him be the glory both now and forever. Amen.".* (2 Pet. 3:18).

About the author ...

John Stewart was born and raised near Winnipeg, Canada. He was drafted by the Pittsburgh Penguins (NHL) and played professional hockey for eight years. He was born again in 1977. After graduating from seminary he served as a pastor for fifteen years. During that time he planted two churches and founded Lamplighters International where he now serves as the executive director of the ministry.

Introduction

The book of Joshua occupies a very important place within the scope of God's revelation to man. The first five books of the Bible (often referred to as the Law, the Law of Moses, or the Pentateuch) provide the account of man's beginning and God's dealing with His people before they entered the land of Promise (modern day Israel and some of the surrounding areas). The Books that follow Joshua reveal the history of God's people after they have settled in the Land. Only the book of Joshua records the details of the physical conquest of the land God promised to the patriarch Abraham.

The book of Joshua derives its name from the principal character, Joshua (Hebrew, *Yehosua*). The name Joshua means "Yahweh (Jehovah) saves" or "Yahweh (Jehovah) is salvation". In the Greek New Testament, Joshua is translated *Iesous* (Acts 7:45 and Heb. 4:8) which is the same name the Savior bore.

Historical Background

God promised Abraham and His descendants a land, a posterity, and a blessing (this promise is known as the Abrahamic Covenant, cf. Gen. 12:1-4; 13:14-17; 15:1-7; 17:1-8). Generations passed and Abraham's descendants had not possessed the land God promised their forefathers. In Egypt, God's people cried out for deliverance from the tyranny of Pharaoh and God sent them Moses. But Moses also died and the people still had not received the Promised Land by the Covenant. The book of Joshua is the official record of God's fulfillment of His promise to Abraham and his descendants.

Date

The book of Joshua begins with the death of Moses (Jos. 1:1) and concludes with the death of Joshua (Jos. 24:29). If the Exodus took place in 1446 BC., as many conservative Old Testament scholars believe, Joshua led the Israelites into Canaan in 1406 BC. (the nation of Israel wandered 40 years in the wilderness, cf. Nu. 14:33-35). The conquest of the Promised Land was completed within five years (Jos. 14:7-10). The other major events of the book of Joshua, the allocation of the Land to the various tribes and Joshua's farewell address to the people, would probably have been completed within two years to prevent the resettling of the Promised Land by heathen nations. Therefore, the book of Joshua likely covers a period of five to ten years of Israel's history.

Purpose and Importance

Although the main purpose of the book of Joshua is to provide an official account of the fulfillment of the Abrahamic Covenant, many spiritual lessons can be learned from this important portion of God's Word. The fulfillment of the Abrahamic Covenant should remind NT believers that God can be trusted to fulfill His promises. Another important truth communicated in Joshua is the righteousness of God. God's intolerance for sin in the lives of heathen nations who spurn His name or in the lives of His choicest servants such as Moses reveals His holiness and His impartial opposition to all iniquity.

Finally, Israel's physical conquest of the land yields many invaluable spiritual lessons for the New Testament Christian. The Promised Land is a place and a picture, not of Heaven, with its promises of a blissful utopia, but of the peace and rest available to those who learn to trust God (cf. Heb. 3:7-19). Even though the ancient battlefields are silent, God's people are still engaged in a life-and-death struggle of their own (cf. Eph. 6:10-18, etc.). The sounds of battle are no longer the clash of ancient weapons of war, but the voices of error and truth heard throughout the corridors of life. Both Joshua and the NT writer of Hebrews remind us that this victory will not be won by the fearful, disobedient, or unbelieving (Heb. 3:18-4:9). Therefore, the book of Joshua is much more than a history of Israel's military conquests - it is God's prescription for spiritual victory for every Christian who wants to possess the promises of God.

Study #1a   God Prepares His Leader

Read - Introduction, Joshua 1:1-9; other references as given.

It has been said that God buries his servants but never His plans. At the beginning of our study of Joshua, God buries one servant (Moses) and commissions another (Joshua) to lead His people to victory.

Introduction.

1.   Why does the book of Joshua occupy such an important place in God's revelation to man?

2.   Joshua's original name was Hoshea which means salvation. Moses changed his name to Joshua when he chose him to be one of the 12 men to spy out the land of Canaan (Nu. 13:16).

   a.   What does the name **Joshua** mean?

   b.   What other person in the New Testament has the name that means Jehovah is salvation?

3.   The book of Joshua is the official record of the detailed fulfillment of the ancient promise or covenant God made to an important Old Testament individual. Please give the name of the original recipient of God's promise, the name by which this covenant is known, and the specific Scripture references where the covenant is located?

4.   What are the three major events recorded in the book of Joshua?

5.   According to the **Introduction** how many years of Israel's history are covered by the book of Joshua?

6.   What important reminder does God's fulfillment of the Abrahamic Covenant provide for New Testament Christians?

7.   The book of Joshua teaches that God can be trusted to keep His promises to His people. In addition to this important truth, list at least two other important spiritual truths taught in the book of Joshua?

8.   Unfortunately, many Christians believe crossing the Jordan River into the Promised Land or Canaan is a picture of the Christian dying and going to Heaven. The familiar Christian song, "On Jordan's Stormy Banks" reads, "Sickness and sorrow, pain and death, are felt and feared no more". However, a survey of Israel's occupation of the Promised Land reveals that sickness, sorrow, pain, and death were not absent from their lives in the Promised Land. If the Promised Land is not a picture of Heaven, what does it represent to the believer?

9. Although New Testament believers are not engaged in physical conflict similar to that experienced by Joshua and Israel, they are engaged in a spiritual battle that threatens to rob them of the peace and rest that comes from trusting God.

    a. If the Christian is not fighting against flesh and blood, whom or what is he fighting against (Eph. 6: 11, 12)?

    b. In this important passage on spiritual warfare (Eph. 6:10-16), there are several words or phrases that assure the believer of victory. Please give at least three phrases that guarantee victory in the Christian life.

    c. What must the Christian do to be victorious in this struggle (Eph. 6:12)?

10. One of the common goals of war is to capture the opponents. What must the Christian take captive if he expects to be victorious in this spiritual battle (2 Cor. 10:3-5)?

"All men desire peace, but very few desire those things which make for peace."

Thomas à Kempis

Study #1b God Prepares His Leader

Read - Joshua 1:1-9; other references as given.

11. Moses led the children of Israel out of bondage in Egypt, delivered the Law of God to them at Mount Sinai, and ministered to their needs during the 40 years of wandering in the wilderness. Moses died at Mount Nebo shortly before the nation of Israel entered the Promised Land. God chose Joshua to succeed Moses as leader of His people.

    a. What word is used to describe both of these great leaders (v. 1)?
       What did Christ say to His disciples about true greatness (Mk. 10:42-45)?

    b. What evidence do you see in your life that you are becoming a servant?

12. Besides being a servant, Joshua demonstrated other character qualities that made him an excellent choice as the new leader of God's people. From the following verses, list several other character qualities that God had developed in Joshua's life (Ex. 17:8-10; 24:12-18; Nu. 13:16-14:9).

13. When God commissioned Joshua as the new leader of His people He gave him three specific promises.

   a. What are they (Jos. 1:2-5)?

   b. In what way(s) do you think these promises would help Joshua be victorious as he led Israel into a hostile land?

   c. In what way has a specific promise from God strengthened your life?

14. While the Abrahamic Covenant was unconditional, Joshua's effectiveness as a leader was conditional upon his obedience to the instructions he was given.

   a. What specific commands was Joshua to obey as he led the people into the land (vv. 6-9)?

    b. Why do you think God repeated some of these instructions to Joshua?

15. There is an important phrase that indicates the type of obedience God expects from everyone who desires to experience His abundant peace and rest (vv. 7, 8).

    a. What is this phrase?

    b. Is there anything in your life that is keeping you from experiencing the peace and rest God wants to give you (e.g., sinful conduct or attitudes such as bitterness, malice, resentment toward another person, etc.)?

16. God promised Joshua success if he was careful to do the things God commanded him (vv. 7, 8). To Joshua, success meant military victory over his enemies and the establishment of the people within the Land.

    a. Success in the church is often measured by the number of people, the size of the church building, etc. What *do you think* is the definition of success within a church ministry?

    b. What *do you think* is a good definition of success in the Christian life?

Study #2a   How To Prepare For Victory

Read - Joshua 1:10-2:24; other references as given.

1. In Israel's history, there was no greater prophet and leader than Moses (De. 34:10-12). As successor to this great servant of God, Joshua must have recognized the awesome responsibility God had given him.

    a. What was Joshua's first action as leader of God's people (vv. 10-11)?

    b. In this first action, Joshua did three important things that helped establish him as an effective leader of God's people. What are they (v. 10)?

2. Moses had previously given the tribes of Reuben, Gad and the half-tribe of Manasseh permission to settle east of the Jordan (Nu. 32:1-20; De. 3:12-20). Joshua reminds them of their responsibility to help the other tribes conquer the Land.

    a. If the participation of the two and a half tribes in the conquest of the Promised Land was not necessary for victory (Note: victory was assured because of God's promise to Joshua, cf. Jos. 1: 5, 6), why was it necessary for them to join the other tribes in battle (Nu. 32:6, 7)?

b. When the two and a half tribes originally requested permission to settle east of the Jordan River, Moses rebuked them by saying, "**Shall your brethren go to war while you sit here?**" (Nu.32:6). In what way(s) do you think a Christian's lack of involvement in the Lord's work affects others who are faithful in their service to God?

c. Do you ever find yourself wanting to sit back in the Christian life and let others do the work of the Lord?

3. During the original discussion with Moses (Nu. 32:1-32), the two and a half tribes volunteered to go before the other tribes into battle (Nu. 32:16, 17) and Moses readily accepted their offer (Nu. 32:20, 21). As they prepared to cross the Jordan, Joshua reminded them of their previous commitment (Jos. 1:14). Why do you think it was important for these tribes to take this lead position during the conquest of the Promised Land?

4. If all the valiant warriors from the two and a half tribes followed Joshua into battle (Jos. 1:14), who protected their wives, their little ones, and their livestock from the hostile nations while they were at war (Nu. 26:1, 2, 7, 19, 34; Jos. 4:12, 13)?

5. The commitment of the tribes of Rueben, Gad, and the half-tribe of Manasseh to submit to Joshua's leadership must have been a great encouragement to him (Jos. 1:16-18).

    a. The tribes made four specific commitments to Joshua (Jos. 1:16-18). What are they?

    b. What did they ask of Joshua (vv. 17, 18)?

    c. When was the last time God used someone's obedience to encourage you?

6. In preparation for the invasion into the Promised Land, Joshua sent spies to gather information. Forty years previously, Moses had sent Joshua and the other spies on a similar mission (cf. Nu. 13:1-14:10). Undoubtedly, Joshua remembered that fateful excursion as he sent out the men (Jos. 2:1). Do you think Joshua's decision to send out the spies represented a lack of faith or wise planning? Why?

7. Ten of the spies sent out by Moses brought back a negative report that discouraged the people (cf. Nu. 13:25-14:4). This negative report caused the people to turn away from the Lord and a majority of them perished in the wilderness. On the second reconnaissance mission, Joshua made some significant changes to prevent a similar problem. Name three specific changes Joshua made for this second spy mission (Nu. 13:1-26; Jos. 2:1, 23).

Study #2b   How To Prepare For Victory

8.   God promised Joshua victory (Jos. 1:3-8) but He did not provide the exact details of how the Land was going to be conquered. Why do you think God provides promises to His people but often reveals the details of His specific plan to them over a long period of time?

9.   Rahab protected the lives of the Israelite spies by deceiving her own countrymen. As in modern times, her actions would be considered an act of treason punishable by death. It appears that her actions were instrumental in saving the lives of the two spies. Some Christians believe there are times in life when lying is admissible (e.g., war, the protection of the innocent, etc.). Other Christians believe lying is always sinful (Ex. 20:16; Eph. 4:25). Do you believe Rahab's lie was excusable because of the circumstances or a sin resulting from her lack of faith (Jos. 2:4-6)?   Why?

10.   Rahab hid the spies beneath the flax stalks on her roof (v. 6). Flax stalks were pulled up during harvest and soaked in water for three to four weeks to separate the fibers. After they were allowed to dry on the flat roofs of the houses, they were made into linen cloth. Why did Rahab risk her life for the protection of these strangers (Jos. 2:9-13)?

11. Rahab is one of only three women who are mentioned in the genealogy of the Lord Jesus Christ (Matt. 1:5, 6). She is enshrined in the "hall of faith" (Heb. 11:31) and used by James to illustrate the importance of works as an evidence of genuine conversion (Ja. 2:25). Give at least three evidences of her genuine conversion (Jos. 2:8-13).

12. The people of Jericho knew Israel had destroyed the Amorites on their way into the Land (v. 10). In many passages of Scripture, the destruction of other heathen nations (in reality, small city-states) is recorded. Often, the only motive that is stated for the destruction is simple obedience to God's command. However, the nature of God's character does not allow Him to arbitrarily destroy people without cause. Why were the Amorites destroyed (Gen. 15:16)?

13. As an immoral person, Rahab was used to destroy lives (cf. Pro. 5:10-14; 6:20-35; 7:6-27). After her conversion, she experienced an immediate desire to preserve life. List all the people that were saved from destruction by her act of faith (Jos. 2:12, 13, 23; 6:22, 23).

14. The spies told Rahab they would spare her and her family if she met three conditions. What were these conditions (Jos. 2:18-20)?

15. Some interpreters of the Bible believe the scarlet cord (v. 18) Rahab was to hang outside her window is a picture of the blood of the Passover lamb that saved the Israelite homes from death during the exodus from Egypt. Others see the scarlet cord as a picture of the blood of Christ that also saves people from destruction. Do you think the scarlet cord was used to simply identify Rahab's residence and protect it from destruction or do you believe the scarlet cord is also a picture of one or both of the things mentioned above?

16. The spies that were sent out by Moses saw giants in the land and returned defeated (Nu. 13:28, 29). The spies sent out by Joshua saw a great fortified city and returned exuberant (Jos. 2:23, 24).

    a. What was the difference (vv. 23, 24)?

    b. Take a few moments to consider the important struggles in your life. As you honestly evaluate your present response to these problems, is your attitude one of defeat and discouragement or joy and anticipation of victory through Christ? Perhaps you could ask a family member for another perspective.

Psalm 119:105 "Your word is a lamp to my feet and a light to my path."

Study #3a   The Importance Of Faith

Read - Joshua 3:1-4:24; other references as given.

1. The book of Joshua is more than a record of ancient Israelite history. It is God's prescription for believers who want to learn to live by faith and experience the rest that comes from trust in God. It has been said that a Christian is either a victor or a victim; a conqueror or a casualty.

    a. A Christian needs only one thing to live victoriously over the world. What is it (1 Jn. 5:4)?

    b. How does the believer gain the faith to overcome the world (Ro. 10:17)?

2. The Israelites were camped at Shittim (approximately seven miles east of the Jordan River) when the two men spied out the Land. What did Joshua and the sons of Israel do when they received the spies' report (Jos. 3:1)?

3. There must have been great anticipation and fear in the hearts of God's people as they camped on the east bank of the Jordan River. No doubt some remembered forty years earlier when Moses had brought them out of Egypt to the edge of the Red Sea.

    a. Why do you think God made them wait at the river's edge before they crossed (vv. 1, 2)?

b. Think of a specific time when you trusted God. What were some of the thoughts and feelings you experienced as you stepped out by faith? (Note: your willingness to share specific details might be a tremendous encouragement to others.)

4. Many of God's people believe salvation is only deliverance from the penalty of sin. Rescued from Egypt, they are willing to spend the remainder of their lives wandering in the wilderness of unbelief and fear.

   a. What reason did Moses give for the deliverance of God's people from the bondage in Egypt (De. 6:23)?

   b. How can Moses' statement, **Then He brought us out from there, that he might bring us in ...,** be applied to the Christian life?

5. The Israelites were not led by elite soldiers but by a group of unarmed Levitical priests carrying the ark of the covenant of the Lord (also called the ark of the Lord or the ark, cf. Jos. 3:13, 15). The ark symbolized God's presence among His people. The people were to keep 2,000 cubits (approximately 1,000 yards) between themselves and the ark. Why were they to keep this distance from the ark (v. 4)?

6. The Israelites were to keep their eyes on the ark as a visible reminder that it was the Lord who was leading them into the Land.

   a. On what or whom should the Christian focus if he wants to live victoriously in this world (Heb. 12:1, 2)?

b. If a Christian wants to live by faith, he must be willing to relinquish or give up two things in his life. What are they (Heb. 12:1)?

c. What is the specific meaning of the word **weight** (Heb. 12:1) and to what does it refer in the Christian's life?

d. Is there anything in your life (sin, weights, encumbrances) hindering your focus on the Lord and keeping you from the rest of faith?
    If there are, why not confess them to the Lord and ask for His forgiveness (cf. 1 Jn. 1:9)?

7. God's people were told to sanctify themselves in anticipation of the manifestation of His miraculous working (Jos. 3:5). In the OT, sanctification or consecration involved bathing, putting on clean clothing, and abstaining from sexual intercourse (cf. Ex. 19:10-15). If the NT believer wants to experience the power of God in his life, what must he put aside and **put on** (Col. 3:8, 14)? (Note: The Greek words for **put off**, [*apekuomai*, to take off completely, to strip off of one's self, v. 8], and **put on**, [*enduomai,* to clothe one's self, v. 10], beautifully identify this passage with the OT regulations for consecration).

Study #3b   The Importance Of Faith

Read - Joshua 3:1-4:24; other references as given.

8.   Joshua told the priests to lead the people across the overflowing Jordan River (v. 6, cf. v. 15). The priests obeyed (v. 14). Joshua told the people to follow the priests (vv. 9-13). The people obeyed (v. 14). Joshua told the priests to step into the Jordan in obedience to God's command. Then God miraculously stopped the waters allowing the people to cross on dry ground.

   a.   Why do you think God waited to demonstrate His power until the last moment?

   b.   From the following verses, give three reasons why God allows His people to experience testing (Ex. 16:4; 20:20; De. 8:16).

9.   Some liberal interpreters have suggested that the stopping of the waters of the Jordan River was simply the result of a natural disaster (such as a landslide caused by an earthquake). Give at least two reasons the stopping of the waters was miraculous (Jos. 3:13-16).

10.   The priests remained in the middle of the riverbed until all the people had crossed over to the other side (Jos. 3:17). What did the Lord command Joshua to do next (Jos. 4:1-5)?

11. The twelve stones were taken from the Jordan, carried approximately six miles, and set up as a memorial at Gilgal which was one and one quarter miles northeast of Jericho (vv. 19, 20; note: Jericho, v. 19, refers to the entire oasis). Why were they set up as a memorial (vv. 6, 7, 19-24)?

12. Next, Joshua set up twelve more stones in the middle of the Jordan River where the priests had stood while the people crossed (Jos. 4:9). The Scriptures do not indicate that God instructed him to set up this memorial or that God condemned his action in any way.

     a. If the stones would soon be covered by the waters of the Jordan, why do you think Joshua set up this "memorial"?

     b. Joshua demonstrated an important leadership principle by this action. What was it?

13. The people trusted God and He showed His power by stopping the waters of the Jordan. Those who passed through the dry riverbed would never forget that day. How did this one act of faith and the demonstration of God's power affect the rest of their lives (Ju. 2:7)?

14. Memorials are important to God's people. For the children of Israel, it was the crossing of the Red Sea, the miraculous provision of food and water in the wilderness, and the crossing of the Jordan. These memorials were vivid reminders of God's faithfulness that motivated them to continue trusting God.

    a. List at least three places God has turned into "faith memorials" as you trusted Him in a time of need.

    b. How does the memory of these victories influence your present walk with God?

15. The Israelites trusted the Lord and entered the Land God had promised them. But even though they were in the Promised Land they still needed to follow the Lord. What are some specific areas in your life in which you need to trust God's guidance and wisdom?

16. The NT instructs us that **whatever things were written before were written for our learning** (Ro. 15:4; cf. 1 Cor. 10:11). What spiritual lessons have you learned from this precious portion of God's Word?

Psalm 119:105 "Your word is a lamp to my feet and a light to my path."

Study #4a   Whose Battle Is It Really?

Read - Joshua 5:1-6:27; other references as given.

1. The terms Amorites and Canaanites (v. 1) are used in a general sense to identify the heathen nations who lived in the mountains (Amorites) and on the coastal plains near the Mediterranean Sea (Canaanites). The use of these two terms indicates that news of the parting of the Jordan and the Israelites' faith had spread throughout ancient Palestine.

    a. What was the reaction of these heathen nations to the report of God's miraculous power and the Israelites entrance into the Land (v. 1)?

    b. Do you think the Israelites were aware that the news of the Lord's parting of the Jordan and their entrance into the land had spread throughout the entire area?   Why?

2. Christians can easily become discouraged when they adopt the idea that the church in general is ineffective as a witness for Jesus Christ. Some of them withdraw themselves from regular fellowship; others attend sporadically or become indifferent to the many ministries and individual needs within the church. Like the sons of Israel, they are unable to see the witness that comes from simple obedience to the Lord.

    a. While it is true that some churches are spiritually dead (cf. Rev. 2, 3), God always raises up believers who are willing to live for Him. How far did the Lord extend the simple faith of the local churches at Rome and Thessalonica (Ro. 16:19; 1 Thess. 1:6-8)?

    b. Do you think the Thessalonian and Roman Christians were aware of the breadth of their witness for Christ prior to Paul's letters?

3. Joshua led the Israelites to Gilgal that was only a short distance from the city of Jericho (Jos. 4:19). Camped at Gilgal with the Jordan behind them and an open plain before them, the Israelites were extremely vulnerable to enemy attack. As they began the actual conquest of the Land, what was the first command they received from the Lord (Jos. 5:2)?

4. Submission of the sons of Israel to national circumcision was more than an inconvenience. It immobilized the entire army forcing the nation to utterly depend on God's mercy.

   a. The nation had just demonstrated their trust in the Lord and had won a great spiritual victory. Why do you think God chose this particular time to give His command?

   b. The timing of this test of faith teaches a valuable spiritual lesson for NT believers who want to live by faith. What is this lesson?

5. It was not surprising that the Lord expected them to be circumcised. What was surprising was the timing of the Lord's command. Describe a recent situation in your life when God allowed your faith to be tested at an unexpected time. Did you respond in faith like the Israelites or did you react negatively (e.g., grumble, dispute with others, etc.)?

6. When God reaffirmed His covenant with Abraham, He promised him the land of Canaan as an inheritance (Gen. 17:7-14). At that time, the Lord warned Abraham that anyone who was not circumcised would be breaking the covenant and cut off from the nation (Gen. 17:10-14). Israel's willingness to submit to circumcision was their acknowledgment that the land was a gift from God and a visible expression of their identification with the Lord in a covenant relationship.

    a. In addition to the physical operation, the words **circumcision** and **uncircumcision** are used symbolically in Scripture. Give three other meanings of the word (Acts 7:51; Ro. 2:28, 29; Col. 2:11, 12)?

    b. If the Promised Land is a picture of the peace and rest God promises to all Christians who are willing to live by faith, what visible expression of identification do you think God expects from NT believers who want to experience His hand of blessing?

7. What do you think is meant by the statement, **"This day have I rolled away the reproach of Egypt from you"** (Jos. 5:9)?

Study #4b   Whose Battle Is It Really?

8. The apostle Paul told the Philippians to forget what lies behind and reach forward to what lies ahead (Phi. 3:13). While this is excellent counsel for many situations in life, God does not want His people to forget His working on their behalf.

   a. What were the Israelites to be reminded of when they observed the Passover (Ex.12:21-28)?

   b. What should NT believers do to help them remember their deliverance from the slavery of sin (1 Cor. 11:23-26)?

9. The timing of Israel's national circumcision and their observance of the Passover feast in the midst of a hostile land are significant. What have you learned about the observance of religious memorials from this passage (Jos. 5:1-1 0)?

10. As the nation camped at Gilgal, Joshua was confronted by an unidentified man. Joshua asked the man if he was with them or against them. To Joshua, there was no middle ground.

    a. What did the man answer (v. 14)?

    b. Who do you think this individual was (cf. Ju. 2:1, 2:6:11-13)?

11. This captain of the host of the Lord said he was neither on Joshua's side nor on the enemies' side. His answer caused Joshua to fall on his face before him (v. 14). What important spiritual lesson did Joshua learn from His answer?

12. All the instruction and preparation in the world would not conquer the Land. The battles would not be fought in the glorious imaginations of men's minds as they sat comfortably around the campfires but on the blood-drenched soil of human suffering. For the Christian, victory is won as temptations and trials are conquered in the power of the Holy Spirit (cf. Gal. 5:16).

   a. The great walled city of Jericho must have looked impenetrable. As the Israelites prepared to attack the great walled city of Jericho, what promise did the Lord give Joshua (Jos. 6:2)?

   b. Unlike Israel, the Christian's struggle is not against flesh and blood (cf. Eph. 6:12). Who or what are some of the Christian's enemies (Acts 20:28-30; Gal. 5:16, 17; Col. 2:8; Heb. 3:11, 12)?

13. The believer's struggle to live victoriously over sin can look hopeless. What promises has God given believers to strengthen them in their struggle (Matt. 28:20; Ro. 8:31, 37; 1 Cor. 10:13; 1 Jn. 1:9)?

14. When the Israelites entered the Land, they set up a memorial (Jos. 4:20-24), submitted to a painful surgery (Jos. 5:2-9), and held a religious celebration (Jos. 5: 10, 11). It is very likely that none of the Israelites could have predicted the events that had taken place shortly after they entered the Land.

   a. How was Joshua to attack Jericho (Jos. 6:2-5)?

   b. Sometimes Christians fail to obey God's commands because they seem strange or unusual. Why do some of God's instructions seem strange to believers (Isaiah 55:8, 9)?

   c. Give a personal example of one of God's commands that seemed unusual at the time but made sense after you stepped out on faith and obeyed.

15. Why do you think God instructed the Israelites to walk around Jericho for seven days?

16. God gave specific instruction to the Israelites that Jericho was under the ban (vv. 17, 18). What did this mean (vv. 17-24)?

Study #5a   Handling Spiritual Defeat

Read - Joshua 7:1-8:35; other references as given.

It has been said that sin will cost you more than you want to pay and take you farther than you want to go. In this lesson, one man's sin brings devastation on himself, his family, and an entire nation.

1. a.   What caused the anger of the Lord to burn against the sons of Israel (v. 1)?

    b.   Why did God hold the entire nation of Israel accountable for the sin of only one man (vv. 11, 15)?

2.   Apparently, Joshua was unaware of Achan's sin when he sent out the spies to investigate the Land (Note: Jericho, v. 2, refers to the plains surrounding the destroyed city, cf. Jos. 5:10). What report did the spies bring back (v. 3)?

3.   After crossing the Jordan and their victory at Jericho, the Israelites must have been confident that they could easily conquer the Land. It appears that Joshua and the other leaders decided to use the old military strategy, "divide and conquer". Heading westward, they planned to divide the Land before their enemies could form a powerful alliance.

a. Satan attempts to cause division among God's people in order to destroy their witness for Christ. Besides being the will of God (cf. Ps. 133; Eph. 4:1-3; Phi. 2:1-3, etc.), what are two other important reasons Christians should strive to live in harmony with one another (Jn. 13:34, 35; 17:20-23)?

b. Whom and what does the devil use to cause division among God's people (Pro. 16:28; Acts 20:28-30; 1 Cor. 1: 10-13; Ro. 14:1-4; Ja. 4:1, 2)?

4. There were three negative results from the first battle against Ai. What were they (Jos. 7:4, 5)?

5. When Joshua heard about the defeat at Ai, he prostrated himself before the ark of the Lord and prayed to God (vv. 6-9; for other ancient expressions of grief, cf. De. 9:18; Jdgs. 20:23; 1 Sam. 7:6). What three things do you notice about Joshua's prayer that made it unacceptable to the Lord (vv. 7-9)?

6. It was Israel's sin and not God's failure that had caused their defeat at Ai and the death of approximately thirty-six men. God promised to bless the nation if they were willing to obey Him according to the Covenant.

a. What two things did God promise the nation if they were not willing to deal with the sin within the camp (vv. 12, 13)?

b.   In what way(s) do you think a believer's unwillingness to forsake sin affects his ability to stand against his enemies (anger, lust, bitterness, immorality, malice, strife, selfishness; for an expanded list of the deeds of the flesh, cf. Gal. 5:19-21)?

7.   The concept of corporate responsibility or spiritual solidarity is not isolated to God's dealing with Israel. In the NT, the apostle Paul gave a strong warning and specific instruction to a local church that was allowing a professing Christian to continue in immoral behavior while he remained part of the fellowship.

    a.   What specific instruction did the apostle Paul give to the Corinthian church regarding this immoral Christian (1 Cor. 5:1-7)?

    b.   Why did the apostle Paul instruct the church at Corinth to remove the man who was persisting in immoral behavior (1 Cor. 5:5-7)?

"Throughout the history of civilization man has shown a complete inability to accurately assess the effects of sin upon himself and others."

Study #5b Handling Spiritual Defeat

Read - Joshua 7:1-8:35; other references as given.

8. When God commanded Joshua to assume leadership of the nation, he obeyed immediately (Jos. 1:10). When He received the report from the spies who went to Jericho, he arose early and moved by faith to the edge of the Jordan (Jos. 3:1).

    a. Joshua and his messengers demonstrated a similar responsiveness when God informed them of Achan's sin. Please give four evidences of their holy hatred for sin (Jos. 7:16, 19, 22, 23, 25)?

    b. Sometimes Christians demonstrate a hatred for sin when they observe sin in the lives of others. Take a few moments to examine your own life. Do you have the same zeal as Joshua did when God reveals sin in your life?

9. In what way(s) do you think a believer's confession of sin can bring glory to God (Jos. 7:19)?

10. When Israel conquered Jericho, Achan could not help seeing the beautiful things left in the city. If seeing the beautiful things was not sinful, how did he sin (Jos. 7:20, 21)?

11.   Prior to the first battle with Ai there is no record of the Lord's instruction to Joshua (cf. Jos. 7:1-4). Only after Israel dealt with Achan's sin did God assure Israel of victory at Ai (Jos. 8:1). If there has been a time in your life when you assumed that God was endorsing your actions but later realized that you were wrong, give some specific details of the situation for the benefit of others in your discussion group.

12.   Although the word ban (Heb. *herem*) is not specifically mentioned in relationship to the conquest of Ai, the concept is present (Jos. 8:1, 2). How did the ban imposed on Ai differ from the one on Jericho (v. 2)?

13.   God explicitly told Joshua to **lay an ambush** (Jos. 8:2) that could be considered a form of deception. Why do you think the Lord's instruction to set the ambush during a time of war was not a violation of the Biblical standard of absolute honesty?

14.   Describe the general details of Joshua's military plan to conquer the city of Ai (Jos. 8:3-13)?

15. Sometime after the defeat of Ai, Joshua led the people thirty miles north to Shechem that lay in the valley between Mount Ebal and Mount Gerizim (v. 30). Why did Joshua build an altar of uncut stones on Mount Ebal (Jos. 8:30, 31; De. 27:1-8)?

16. A copy of the Law of Moses was to be written on some large stones. This difficult task was performed in the sight of all Israel (Jos. 8:32).

     a. What effect do you think the writing of the Law of Moses on stone had on Joshua?

     b. What effect do you think Joshua's writing of the law of Moses had on the people (especially the children) as they watched him?

     c. In what ways do you think a spiritual leader's commitment to the Word of God influences others (note: this could include a parent, Sunday School teacher, etc.)?

17. After Joshua had written the Law of Moses on the stones, he assembled the people and read the Law to them. This is the third formal reading of the Law of Moses (Note: Moses first gave God's Law to the Israelites at Mt. Sinai, Ex. 19 ff., and then repeated the Law on the plains of Moab, the book of Deuteronomy). Half the people were assembled on the slope of Mount Ebal while the other half of the people were assembled on the slope of Mount Gerizim (Jos. 8:32). As Joshua read the Law of Moses, what things do you observe about this important event (vv. 34, 35)?

Study #6a   The Enemy's Secret Weapon

Read - Joshua 9:1-27; other references as given.

1. Fresh from their victories over Jericho and Ai and the third formal giving of the Law at Shechem, the Israelites turned south to possess the land of promise. Who were their new enemies (Jos. 9:1, 2)?

2. The Land was a gift from God but it had to be won by physical conquest. Some Christians say, "Let go and let God". They appear to be waiting for some personal revelation from God in order to do His will. At the other end of the spiritual spectrum are those Christians who believe the Christian life is simply the dutiful fulfillment of an endless series of religious obligations (cf. Gal. 3:1-3). What is the proper Biblical balance for a Christian between trusting God and personal responsibility (Col. 1:29)?

3. The kings of the southern city-states formed an alliance against Israel. The sons of Israel would no longer be able to conquer the land one city at a time. Not only did the easy victories of the past give way to greater challenges in the present, but this organized resistance offered them greater potential for victory and rapid advancement within the Promised Land.

    a. Some Christians are afraid to trust God because they think living by faith will only bring greater spiritual challenges. Perhaps they have observed a dedicated believer experiencing a tremendous trial. Are you afraid to live by faith because you think God might allow you to experience something that is more than you can bear?

    b.   If a Christian lives by faith he also experiences greater opportunities in his walk with God. Name at least three?

4.   The power of the Lord was witnessed to Rahab and she turned to Him in faith (cf. Jos. 2:8-11). The power of the Lord was witnessed to the kings of the south and they prepared to fight the people of God (Jos. 9:1, 2). How did the Gibeonites respond to this same witness of the power of God (vv. 3-13)?

5.   The Gibeonites acted craftily because they had heard of **His fame** (i.e., the Lord; Heb. *sem*; name or character of a person, v. 9). Please list four words you believe best describe the character of God beginning with the word that you think most accurately describes His nature (e.g., mercy, holy, patient, etc.).

6.   The men of Gibeon pretended to be from a very far country (v. 9). In reality, they lived only twenty miles west of the Israelites' camp at Gilgal.

    a.   What did the Gibeonites want from Joshua and the Israelites (vv. 6, 11)?

    b.   What three things did the Gibeonites do in order to deceive the Israelites (vv. 7-13)?

7. The NT teaches that Satan disguises himself as an angel of light as he works through ungodly men (cf. 2 Cor. 11:14, 15). Throughout the NT Christians are warned to be wary of these deceitful workers and to not allow them to promote their heresy within the church (cf. 1 Tim. 1:3-7). Name several of Satan's servants whom he uses to accomplish his wicked schemes (Acts 20:28-30; 2 Cor. 11: 12-15; 2 Pet. 2:1-4).

8. The Gibeonites acted wisely by not mentioning anything about Israel's recent defeats of Jericho and Ai. Their deception was obviously well planned and enough to entice Joshua to enter into a covenant with them (v. 15). There are at least two important reasons why Joshua and the men of Israel failed to avoid this unholy alliance. What are they (Ex. 34:12; Pro. 18:13, 17; Jos. 9:14)?

9. Why did the Lord command the Israelites not to make any covenants with the inhabitants of the land (Ex. 34:12)?

"Saying yes to God means saying no to those things that offend His holiness".

Study #6b   The Enemy's Secret Weapon

10. God's prohibition against unholy alliances is repeated in the New Testament (cf. 2 Cor. 6:14). The apostle Paul emphasizes this important Biblical teaching by incorporating five vivid comparisons into several rhetorical questions (2 Cor. 6:14-16). In each of these comparisons, he uses a different word to show the impossibility of spiritual unity between a Christian and a non-Christian.

    a. Complete the following sentence using these five key words. The Christian can have no real _____ or _____ or _____ or _____ or _____ with a non-Christian.

    b. In an earlier letter to the same church, Paul had to clarify that separation from the world did not mean adopting an isolationist attitude (cf. 1 Cor. 5:9-11). If Christians are not to become isolationists, what are some specific circumstances in which you think a believer should not be unequally yoked together with unbelievers?

    c. Even the great spiritual leader Joshua was enticed into an unholy alliance. What spiritual decisions do you think Christians should make to guard themselves against becoming trapped in unholy alliances?

11. Three days after Joshua and the men of Israel had made a covenant with the men of Gibeon, they learned about the true identity of the impostors (Jos. 9:16).

    a. How did the whole congregation respond when they learned about the leaders' error (v. 18)?

    b. Why couldn't Joshua and the leaders destroy the Gibeonites when they learned that the oath was based upon the Gibeonites' deceitfulness (v. 18)?

12. Joshua and the leaders made a critical mistake by entering into an unholy alliance with the Gibeonites. However, Joshua and the leaders acted wisely by doing several things that prevented the compounding of the problem and the judgment of God. Please list at least four (Jos. 9:18-21).

13. Joshua and the men of Israel kept their word even though their promise was based upon the Gibeonites' lies. Many years later, King Saul violated Joshua's oath to the Gibeonites and brought judgment on Israel. God's people are instructed to avoid making false oaths or swearing about future events over which they have no control (cf. Matt. 5:33-37; Ja. 5:12). They are also commanded to keep their word (Ecc. 5:4-6). Do you think a Christian is obligated to fulfill his word to those who use deceit during the original negotiations of an agreement (e.g., marriage, the purchase of a car, house, a commitment to an employer, etc.)? Why)?

14. If a believer is obligated to keep his word, what precautions would you recommend regarding entering into agreements (business contracts, leases, etc.) with other people?

15. At first glance, Joshua's question seems somewhat naive (Jos. 9:22). Why do you think he confronted the Gibeonites when he could assume their actions were motivated by a desire to preserve the lives of their people (vv. 22-25)?

16. There are several important truths about living for God in this ninth chapter of Joshua. The apostle Paul said **Now all these things happened to them as examples, and they were written for our admonition (1 Cor. 1O:11).** List two spiritual truths you learned from this chapter and restate them as personalized life principles (e.g., When I sin or make a mistake, I will admit my error, accept the disapproval of others, not sin to cover my mistake and make the best out of the situation, cf. Jos. 9:18-21).

Congratulations. You have just completed Joshua Part One. We hope your study of this exciting portion of God's Word has helped you understand some of the biblical principles for spiritual victory. In the second part of Joshua, the combined Israelite army conquers the main resistance in the land but leaves the final conquest of the land to the various tribes. Each tribe must conquer their individual enemies before they can live in peace and inherit God's promised blessings. The successes and failures of the individual tribal conquests reveal some very powerful truths about spiritual conflict, faith and inheriting God's blessing. We hope that you will continue your study of Joshua so you can discover these truths and possess the rich inheritance that God promises every believer.

#1   God Prepares His Leader

1. Joshua is the only Old Testament book that records the details of the physical conquest of the land God promised to Abraham and his descendants.

2. a. Yahweh (Jehovah) saves or Yahweh (Jehovah) is salvation.
    b. Jesus.

3. Abraham; the Abrahamic Covenant; Gen. 12:14, 13:14-17, 15.1-7, 17.1-8.

4. The conquest of the Land, the allocation of the Land to the various tribes of Israel, and the farewell addresses of Joshua.

5. Five to ten years.

6. If God was faithful to keep His promises to ancient Israel, He will be faithful to fulfill His promises to NT believers.

7. The book of Joshua teaches God is righteous. This is made evident by His unwillingness to tolerate sin wherever it is found. Second, the book of Joshua teaches several principles of spiritual warfare.

8. The Promised land pictures the place in the Christian's life where he learns to live by faith in God. The writer of Hebrews calls it the "rest'" (cf. Heb. 3:7-19) because the term reflects the quietness of the soul the believer experiences when he learns to trust God for every provision of life.

9. a. He is fighting against the wiles of the devil, principalities, powers, the rulers of the darkness, spiritual hosts of wickedness in the heavenly places.
    b. "… you may be able to stand against" (v. 11), "to withstand" (v. 13), "to stand" (v. 13), "be able to quench all the fiery darts of the wicked one" (v. 16).
    c. He must grow or mature in his relationship with Christ ("put on the whole armor of God") to the point that he is able to withstand the attacks of Satan. While the believer is the recipient of the grace of God at salvation (cf. Ti. 3:5, etc.), he is commanded to continue in the grace that is made available to him (i.e., the power of the Holy Spirit) and the instruction of the Word (cf. Jn. 8:32; 17:17). He must take active steps to insure spiritual advancement (cf. 2 Pet. 1:5-10). He is to "put on" (Greek, *enduomai*, to clothe oneself -an imperative or command) truth; v. 14), righteous living or conduct. (Note: this is a reference to practical righteousness or moral excellence because the believer cannot put on

his own salvation (v. 14), peace (v. 15), faith (v. 16), assurance of salvation (v. 17), and the Word of God (v. 17). If the believer puts these things on, he will be spiritually mature (Eph. 6:11, 13).

10. He must allow the Word of God to be the ultimate authority in life. If there are thoughts or reasonings in his thinking that are contrary to the Word of God, he must surrender these reasonings to the authority of the Scriptures no matter how "right" or "logical" they seem. The Greek words the apostle Paul uses in 2 Cor. 10:3-5 depict a military conflict in which the prisoners (in this case erroneous thoughts) are taken captive so that they cannot cause further trouble.

11. a. Slave. If a man wants to be great, he should be the slave of all (Mk. 10:42-45).
    b. Answers will vary.

12. He was a man of courage and obedience (Ex. 17:8-10). He was a man of faith and patience because he waited for Moses for 40 days on the mountain (Ex. 24:12-18). He was a man of faith in God as he could see past the circumstances that appeared overwhelming to others (Nu. 13:16-14:9). He was a man of exceptional character who was able to stand against the majority when they were not willing to trust God (Nu. 13:16-14:9).

13. a. 1. God said He would give them the Land (vv. 3, 4).
       2. God said that no man (i.e., no army) would be able to defeat them as long as Joshua lived, as long as they obeyed Him (v. 5).
       3. God would be with them and He would not fail them or forsake them (v. 5).
    b. 1. Joshua would soon be faced with the pressures of leading a large mass of people into a hostile land. The normal pressures of meeting the needs of the nation could easily cause Joshua to forget that God would not forsake or fail him.
       2. There would be those within the group who would question and resist Joshua's decisions. Joshua needed to be reminded that it was God who was going before him and his responsibility was not so much to lead the people as it was to follow the Lord and the people would then follow his example.
       3. Israel was a traveling nation and not a hardened army. Many of the nations they were about to face presented a formidable enemy for Israel and Joshua needed to be assured of victory through God's provision. No doubt he felt responsible for the safety and welfare of the nation and needed to be assured of victory.
    c. Answers will vary.

14. a. 1. He was to be strong and of good courage (vv. 6, 7, 9).
      2. He was to be very careful to obey all that God had commanded him through Moses (i. e. the Law).
      3. He was to make sure that his responsibilities as leader of God's people did not allow him to be sidetracked (turned to the right or the left, v. 7). In order to do this, he was to meditate on the Word of God and not allow the truth to get away from his thinking.

    b. In an attempt to fulfill his many responsibilities, Joshua might have been easily tempted to forget the promises of God. The pressures of leading the nation and the responsibility of protecting them could have caused him to play it safe and never enter the Land. The repetition of the promises strengthened Joshua to press on in the midst of the normal temptations to the contrary.

15. a. "according to all that is written in it".
    b. Answers will vary.

16. a. The measure of success of a church ministry is not determined by the number of people or the size of the facilities. Christ's assessment of the seven churches in the book of Revelation (cf. Rev. 2, 3) does not mention the size of the congregations. Success in a church ministry is determined by the devotion of the congregation to the Lord. The church at Ephesus (Rev. 2:1-7) was rebuked because they had left their first love (i.e., their love for Christ). The church was busy serving (v. 2) and had separated itself from the world and false teachers (v. 2). However, they were told to repent (v. 5). A church body that makes devotion to Christ their ultimate goal is successful in the eyes of the Lord regardless of the size of the congregation.

    b. A believer is successful in the Christian life if he maintains a dynamic personal love for the Lord Jesus Christ. If a Christian learns to make this His first priority, he will begin to do the things that are pleasing to God. Christ said, "If you love me, you will keep (Greek-future tense) my commandments" (Jn. 14:15). The Christian is tempted to put service before devotion. He wants to show his love for God by his willingness to keep the commandments. But the Christian's love is shown by his desire to maintain a close personal communion with Christ and fruitful service will be the natural by-product.

2   How To Prepare For Victory

1. a. He commanded the officers to instruct the people to prepare themselves to enter the Promised Land.
   b. 1. He responded immediately to the Lord's command. The word "then" refers to his immediate response to the Word of the Lord. He modeled obedience that gave him the authority to expect the same from the people.
      2. He fulfilled the Lord's command to be strong and courageous by commanding instead of asking the officers to obey. The nation needed confident leadership and Joshua assumed the position of authority the Lord had given him.
      3. He worked through the existing authority structure (he commanded the officers of the people). Joshua led Israel by leading the leaders Moses and the people had chosen. Joshua led by example (his obedience), by assuming the authority God had given him and by sharing the administrative responsibilities with others who were capable.

2. a. It was necessary for these tribes to join the other tribes in battle so that the other tribes would not become discouraged (Nu. 32:7).
   b. A believer who is unwilling or reluctant to participate in the work of the Lord has a similar negative effect on other believers who are actively serving the Lord. It is true that God's servants should learn to focus on the joy of serving their Savior, personal experience and the testimonies of faithful Christians and of the Scripture (cf. Phil. 2:19-21, etc.) provide ample proof of the negative effects some believers have on those who are faithful to God.
   c. Answers will vary.

3. If the two and a half tribes had not taken the lead in the battle, it would have been very easy for dissension and strife to develop among the other tribes. The entire twelve tribes had been responsible for conquering the land east of the Jordan River that was given to the two and a half tribes. During this conquest of Trans-Jordania, the other tribes risked their lives to conquer a land they would not inherit. It would be very easy for the two and a half tribes to not fight as intensely because they had already inherited their land. Joshua wanted the nation to function as a unified whole both during and after the conquest of the Land.

4. The 40,000 valiant men (Jos. 4:12, 13) were only a portion of the approximately 110,000 men capable of bearing arms (Nu. 26). Joshua seems to make a distinction between valiant warriors and the men who are capable of going to war (Jos. 1:14). Perhaps these valiant warriors were the most elite soldiers from these tribes or ones who were unencumbered by family responsibilities and willing to participate in an extended military campaign.

5. a. 1. They would obey every command Joshua gave them (v. 16).
      2. They would go wherever he sent them (v. 16).
      3. They would respect and obey Joshua just as they had respected and obeyed Moses (v. 17).
      4. They would not tolerate any form of rebellion within their tribes (v. 18).
      5. They would assume the responsibility of self discipline (v. 18).
   b. They asked him to walk with the Lord ("Only the Lord your God be with you", v. 17) and "to be strong and of good courage (v. 18).
   c. Answers will vary.

6. Wise planning. God provided Joshua with the promise of victory but not the details of the conquest. Joshua and the other leaders were responsible to follow God's specific plan as He revealed it to them. The Scriptures endorse careful preparation as long as it does not become a deterrent to living by faith (cf. Pro. 15:22; 16:9; 20:18; 21:5; Lu. 14:28-31).

7. 1. He chose two spies instead of twelve.
   2. He sent them out secretly (Jos. 2:1).
   3. The spies reported directly to Joshua and were not given the opportunity to influence the people directly (Jos. 2:23).

8. It is God's desire that His people learn to walk in dependence on Him. The progressive unfolding of His plan to His servants fulfills this purpose. God uses man's dependence on Him as a witness to the world.

9. Rahab's lie was a sin resulting from a lack of faith. The Biblical passages that address the subject of truth-telling provide absolutely no exceptions (cf. Ex. 20:16, Eph. 4:25, etc.). The argument that says Rahab's lie was instrumental for the preservation of the lives of the spies fails to acknowledge the sovereignty of God. God did not need her to lie to protect the lives of His two servants. The argument that teaches lying is admissible when a higher good is accomplished promotes the concept that God is glorified by sin. The apostle Paul emphatically argued against this perspective in the book of Romans (cf. Ro. 6:1 ff). God's people have not been called to pragmatic relativism but to unconditional obedience for the glory of God. However, it is important to note that Rahab's action of lying was understandable (although it was still a sin) in light of her newfound faith and the severity of the circumstances. The Scriptures emphasize (and believers should as well) the

courage and faith she demonstrated in the midst of a life and death struggle (cf. Heb. 11:31; Ja. 2:25).

10. Rahab's actions were entirely motivated by the fear of the Lord (vv. 9-12). It is interesting to note that Rahab was not given any more revelation than the rest of the people of Jericho but she alone responded to the truth God revealed to her. In the book of Hebrews, the writer clearly identifies Rahab as a woman of faith and identifies the rest of the people of Jericho as disobedient (an obvious indication of their own failure to respond to the truth, Heb. 11:31). It is also interesting to note that God is continually bringing others to Himself in salvation.

11. 1. Her belief in the power of the Lord (v. 9).
    2. Her clear testimony of belief in the person of the Lord (He is God, v. 11).
    3. Her willingness to risk her life to preserve the lives of others (cf. Ja. 2:25).
    4. Her genuine fear of the Lord motivated her actions (v. 11).

12. Since the days of Abraham, God was aware of their sin. God used the nation of Israel to be His instrument of judgment because they had failed to repent. The judgment of the Amorites demonstrates the patience and grace of God.

13. In addition to herself, her act of faith saved her father, mother, brothers, sisters and their families (Jos. 2:13). The two spies were also saved by her faith (Jos. 2:21).

14. Rahab had to hang a scarlet cord in the same window of her house by which the spies escaped. (v. 18). Secondly, all of her family had to be in her house at the time of the battle (v. 18). Thirdly, she could not tell anyone about the pact that was made between her and the spies (v. 20).

15. The scarlet cord was used to simply identify her residence and protect her from destruction. The Scriptures make no mention of the scarlet cord being a symbol or type of the blood of the Passover lamb or the blood of Christ. Although the Scriptures use certain things as types (e.g., the Passover lamb pictured the ultimate sacrifice of Jesus Christ cf. Jn. 1:29), students should be careful that they do not go too far and see a type in every text. Seeing a double meaning in every Biblical text is what is known as allegorical interpretation and often leads students to misinterpret the plain meaning of the passage. Remember this simple rule: "If the plain sense (of the passage) makes common sense, seek no other sense".

16. a. The two spies were able to see the Lord in the midst of the circumstances.
    b. Answers will vary.

#3   The Importance of Faith

1. a.   Faith in God.
    b.   The believer must submit himself to the Word of God (hearing the Word).

2. They rose early the next day and moved their camp to the eastern edge of the Jordan.

3. a.   Perhaps God wanted them to contemplate their inability to cross the overflowing Jordan without His intervention. As they camped beside the river, the Israelites must have wondered how they were going to navigate the rapidly flowing waters of the Jordan. For approximately two million people to cross the river would have placed the people at great risk. Waiting at the river's edge would increase their anticipation before the miracle and their appreciation for the Lord.
    b.   Answers will vary.

4. a.   God brought them out of Egypt so that He might bring them into the land He had promised Abraham.
    b.   The believer has not only been saved from slavery to sin but he has also been saved to possess the riches of Christ. Unfortunately, some believers live as if God's only purpose for saving them was to have them wander in the wilderness of fear and unbelief until they enter glory. God not only wants His children to be saved from the bondage of sin but also to experience the fullness of Christ through trust in Him.

5. The people were instructed to keep away from the ark so that everyone could see the priests carrying it. This procedure provided direction for the people and helped them remember that the Lord was leading them into the Land.

6. a.   Jesus Christ.
    b.   The Christian must be willing to give up all sin in his life and anything else that might hinder him from following the Lord (weights or encumbrances).
    c.   A burden, an impediment, a hindrance. In the Christian life, a weight is anything that hinders the believer as he endeavors to live for God. This could include things that are not sinful by nature but become sin to the believer because they cause his attention and focus to be drawn away from the Lord.
    d.   Answers will vary.
          Answers will vary.

7. He must put aside anger, wrath, malice, blasphemy, filthy language, (v. 8), lying (v. 9). He must put on tender mercies, kindness, humility, meekness (v. 12), bearing with one another, long-suffering, forgiveness (v. 13), love (v. 14).

8. a. God often waits to demonstrate His power in the lives of His people to increase their faith and dependence on Him.
    b. 1. To test them to see if they would obey God (Ex. 16:4).
        2. To teach them to fear God (Ex. 20:20).
        3. To teach them to stay away from sin (Ex. 20:20).
        4. To teach them to do good (De. 8:16).

9. 1. The stopping of the waters of the Jordan was predicted before it happened. Natural disasters are usually not predicted.
    2. All the people knew in advance the specific time the waters would be stopped (v.13) and the waters stopped at the exact time (vv.15, 16).
    3. The waters were stopped from above and below (v. 16). If it had been a natural disaster the waters would be stopped on only one side.

10. Twelve men, one from each tribe, were to go back into the river and take twelve stones from the very place where the priests were standing and bring them up to the west side of the river.

11. The twelve stones served as a sign and a memorial for future generations to teach them that God had miraculously parted the waters of the Jordan (vv. 6, 7). The memorial stones were also a reminder for the adults to tell their children about the miracle.

12. a. Joshua was honoring the priests who had demonstrated tremendous faith when they stepped into the flooding Jordan. They had also stood in the river all the time the people passed through the river.
    b. 1. A leader should never cease to be a servant.
        2. A leader should seek ways to show his appreciation for those who have served and sacrificed for the advancement of others.

13. They served the Lord all the rest of their lives but they failed to lead the following generation to salvation (Ju. 2:10). Perhaps they were too busy establishing themselves in the Land to communicate the message of salvation to their children.

14. a. Answers will vary.
    b. Answers will vary.

15. Answers will vary.
16. Answers will vary.

4   Whose Battle Is It Really?

1. a.   The Amorites and the Canaanites had lost courage and were terrified of the Israelites.

    b.   No. The permeation of fear throughout the heathen nations would force the nations to protect themselves as much as possible. In order to do this, they would need to prevent the spread of privileged information about the number and quality of their military force and the general morale of the soldiers. The nations would attempt to accomplish this difficult task by restricting the access and egress to the fortified city to which the citizens had fled (cf. Jos. 6:1). It is fairly certain that the Israelites were not aware of the paralyzing fear that had spread throughout the land.

2. a.   1.   Rome. Paul said the faith of the Roman church had spread to all. More than likely, it is a reference to the entire Christian community throughout the Roman empire (i.e. the various churches) rather than the entire nation. However, in light of the difficulties of ancient transportation and long distance communication, this is a remarkable witness.

        2.   Thessalonica. Their testimony had spread from the church throughout the province in which they ministered (Macedonia; 1 Thess. 1:8). The testimony of the church had also spread south to the neighboring province of Achaia (v. 8). It is interesting that their testimony for the Lord had spread to such an extent that Paul said he did not need to say anything in the entire region.

    b.   Answers will vary.

3.   The Lord commanded them to make flint knives and circumcise the men of Israel.

4. a.   The Israelites were about to inherit the Land God had promised them within the Abrahamic Covenant. This covenant gift could not be accepted by the nation if they were not willing to receive circumcision. Circumcision was a visible expression of their willingness to submit to God and evidence that they understood the land was a gift from God.

    b.   Some of the most severe spiritual tests come immediately after some of the greatest spiritual victories.

5.   Answers will vary.

6. a. 1. The word is used to signify a stubborn resistance to spiritual truth (Acts 7:51).
          2. When the word "circumcision" is qualified by the phrases, "who is one inwardly (Ro. 2:28, 29), "made without hands" or "of Christ" (Col. 2:11, 12) the word signifies salvation.
    b. Baptism by immersion.

7. It probably means that the Israelites, now about to be established in the Land of Promise, had been delivered from the national disgrace of enslavement and homelessness they had experienced in Egypt.

8. a. They were to be reminded of the time when the Lord passed over their homes when He smote the Egyptians and spared their families (Ex. 12:27).
    b. They should partake of the Lord's Supper (also called the Lord's Table or communion).

9. The observance of religious memorials is very important. The timing and location of Israel's observance (a hostile land under the imminent threat of attack) indicates that God is desirous for His people to participate in regular observances of religious memorials.

10. a. "No".
     b. The man said that He was captain of the host (armies) of the Lord. Likely, the pre-incarnate person of Jesus Christ or the angel of the Lord (cf. Ex. 3:2-17; Ju. 6: 11-13). Notice that Joshua fell on his face, bowed down and submitted to His authority. Although it is true that men in that culture often prostrated themselves before men of authority, the passage gives strong indication that this stranger was more than a mere man. The man told Joshua to remove his sandals because he was standing on holy ground. This property was made holy by the presence of this Holy One.

11. As commander-in-chief of Israel, Joshua had assumed the authority God had given him. However, as they prepared to conquer the Land, Joshua needed to be reminded that he was serving God instead of thinking it was God who was helping him. The famous missionary to China, Hudson Taylor, said, "When I first went to China, I asked God to help me with my work. After some time I prayed that I would be able to help God in His work. I finally came to the place where I asked the Lord to do His work through me."

12. a. The Lord promised to give Jericho, its king, and its valiant soldiers into his hand.
     b. 1. Theological error (perverse things, Acts 20:30) taught by ungodly men.
          2. Man's own sinful nature (the flesh, Gal. 5:16, 17).
          3. Humanistic philosophies (Col. 2:8).
          4. Unbelief and other sin (Heb. 3:11, 12).

13. God will never abandon the believer (Matt. 28:20). The Christian can live victoriously over sin (Ro. 8:31, 37). God will never allow the Christian to face more temptation than he is able to bear (1 Cor. 10:13). God promises to forgive all the believer's sin and cleanse him of all unrighteousness (1 Jn. 1:9).

14. a. All the men of war and seven priests were to circle the city once each day for six days and return to camp. On the seventh day the men were to march around the city seven times. After the seventh time, the priests were to blow a long blast on the ram's horns. When the men heard the sound of the ram's horns they were to shout a great shout and the walls would then fall down flat. The soldiers were then instructed to go straight into the city and conquer it.
    b. God's thoughts are higher than man's thoughts. Man's ability to reason correctly is also affected by sin and God's ways are naturally resisted by him.
    c. Answers will vary.

15. The people of Jericho had heard the testimony of the Lord's working in Israel's midst (Jos. 2:9-11). Perhaps the seven-day vigil was another attempt to reach the people of Jericho. Rahab, the harlot, had already turned to God for salvation and the daily spectacle must have been used in the lives of others. The blowing of the ram's horn was a daily reminder that victory was insured.

16. The ban (Heb. herem) meant someone or something was completely and irrevocably consecrated or devoted to God so that it could not be redeemed (cf. Lev. 27: 28, 29). The ban or curse was administered in various degrees (cf. De. 13: 16; 20:10-18; 1 Sam. 15:3). In this case, Jericho and its inhabitants were under the severest form of the ban - one devoted to destruction. While the implementation of the ban on an entire nation (Jericho; an ancient city-state) appears to be extremely harsh, it is important to remember that God had endured the wickedness of the Canaanites of this area (Amorites) for many generations (cf. Gen. 15:16).

#5   Handling Spiritual Defeat

1. a. Achan stole some things during the defeat of Jericho.
    b. Israel was held responsible by God because they were a covenant nation (vv. 11, 15). This does not mean that God did not judge individual sin (e.g., Achan).

2. The city of Ai was not very big so only two or three thousand soldiers needed to go up against the city in battle.

3. a. 1. If Christians love one another, the world (i.e., the unsaved) will be able to tell that they are true followers of Christ (Jn. 14:34, 35). In a world where religious impostors abound, the love of God's people for one another is a powerful tool in God's hand.

          2. If believers live in fellowship with God and in harmony with one another, they will bear witness that Jesus Christ came in the flesh and loved them (Jn. 17:20-23).

    b. 1. Slander (a perverse man, Pro. 16:28).

          2. Ungodly men who cause division within local churches by enticing believers away from the church and encouraging them to follow them (Acts 20:28-30).

          3. Immature believers who place a priority on a specific aspect of the Christian ministry and make adherence to their single priority a test of fellowship (1 Cor. 1:10-13). Paul rebuked the Corinthian Christians because there were four factious groups within the congregation that were causing division (v. 12). The four groups represent a sample of four different ministry approaches or theological perspectives:

              a). those who over emphasize service or grace, "I am of Paul",

              b). those who over emphasize pulpit eloquence or teaching, "I am of Apollos", (cf. Acts 18:24),

              c). those who overemphasize tradition, "I am of Cephas" (those who emphasize tradition over truth; Peter represented the established church in Jerusalem),

              d). those who were falsely pietistic felt they were on a higher spiritual plane than the others in the church, "I am of Christ". Paul rebuked all four groups for their divisive spirit and told them they were acting just like the unsaved (cf. 1 Cor. 3:1-5).

          4. A critical spirit toward other believers because they hold different personal convictions (Ro. 14:14).

          5. The unrestrained lusts of God's people coupled with an unwillingness to pray and trust God for those needs (Ja. 4:1, 2).

4. 1. The Israelite army was defeated (v. 4).

    2. Approximately thirty-six soldiers were killed (v. 5).

    3. The nation of Israel lost courage (v. 5).

5. 1. He questioned God's intentions when he asked if He had only brought the Israelites into the Land to destroy them (v. 7).

    2. Joshua failed to believe God's promises when he said that they should have been willing to dwell east of the Jordan (v. 7).

3. Joshua was more concerned about Israel's reputation and safety than God's name. As leader of Israel, Joshua's concern for the safety of the people was admirable. However, if he had trusted God to fulfill His promises, he would have been able to focus more on Israel's failure than assuming God had failed them - a common error believers make.

6. a. 1. God would not be with them (v. 12). This meant that the Lord would not guide them as they attempted to conquer the Land and He would not go before them by placing fear in the hearts of their enemies.
    2. The Israelites would not be able to stand before their enemies (vv. 12, 13). In other words, they would not be given victory over their enemies as long as they deliberately violated the covenant.

    b. When a believer is unwilling to forsake his sin, this indicates that he has chosen to be a friend of the world instead of a friend of God. By his own choice, the believer becomes an enemy of God (cf., Ja. 4:4) and begins to experience His opposition (Ja. 4:6). The resistance he experiences from God could include the lack of peace, joy, assurance of salvation, etc. Because God's grace is given to the humble (and a believer who persists in sinful conduct is not humble), grace is withdrawn from the sinning believer leaving him powerless to live victoriously over sin. The result is often an increase of sinful behavior coupled with spiritual defeat and guilt.

7. a. The man should be removed from the fellowship (vv. 2, 7). The apostle Paul's statement presupposes the man was unwilling to repent.
    b. If sin of this nature was allowed to continue in the church, it would eventually ruin the church (v. 6).

8. a. 1. Joshua arose early in the morning to deal with the sin in the camp (v. 16).
    2. Joshua implored (v. 19, "I beg you ", Heb. *no*, entreaty or exhortation, cf. Nu. 20:10).
    3. Joshua's messengers ran to Achan's tent (v. 22).
    4. The messengers laid out the stolen property as if they were afraid to handle the things under the ban lest they fall under judgment (v. 23).
    5. They stoned Achan (Jos. 7:25).

    b. Answers will vary.

9. When a believer obeys the Word of God, the Lord is glorified. Because believers are commanded to confess their sin to God (1 Jn. 1:9) and to those against whom they have sinned (Matt. 5:23, 24), their genuine confession of sin glorifies God.

10. He coveted them and took them.

11. Answers will vary.

12. The city and its inhabitants were to be destroyed but the spoil and the cattle could be used by the Israelites. Oh, if Achan had only waited.

13. During a time of war, the opposing armies expect their opponent to use normal military strategy; deployment of troops as decoys, etc. The use of such tactics does not violate the Biblical standard of honesty because there is no assumed trust.

14. Joshua was to send some Israelite soldiers out at night (v. 3) to hide on the north side of the city. He sent some other soldiers on the other side (v. 4) so they could eventually ambush the city. He would feign an attack with the first army and then pretend to flee from the men of Ai as they had during the first battle. When the men of Ai had left the city and pursued the Israelites, Joshua would signal for the second army to attack the city and burn it.

15. Joshua was fulfilling a command the Lord had given the nation through Moses while the Israelites were on the other side of the Jordan.

16. a. This difficult task would have afforded Joshua ample time to think about the Law. This would allow him to meditate on the blessings and the curses and motivate him to lead the nation in the ways of righteousness. Other answers could apply.
    b. Likely, the people would be encouraged in their commitment to the authority of the Law. Other answers could apply.
    c. A spiritual leader is able to exert a powerful influence in the lives of those to whom he ministers. When a spiritual leader is committed to the Word of God, those who follow him are encouraged to make the Word of God a priority in their lives. If a spiritual leader consistently applies the Word of God, he demonstrates that the truth of God's Word is a living pattern for them to follow. Other answers could apply.

17. The Scriptures emphasize that Joshua read all the words of the Law (vv. 34, 35). He did not choose only the portion that spoke of the blessings or the curses. All the people (men, women, children, strangers, i.e., Gentile converts) listened to Joshua as he read the Law.

#6   The Enemy's Secret Weapon

1. The Hittites, Amorites, Canaanites, Perizites, Hivites and Jebusites. (Note: the terms, Amorites and Canaanites, are used in v. 2 to designate the specific city states as compared to the general use of the terms in Joshua 5:1).

2. The Christian must exercise initiative in his walk with God. He must be willing to exert himself for the cause of Christ. However, this labor must not be in the arm of the flesh but according to the grace or power of God (cf. Gal. 5:16).

3. a. Answers will vary.
    1. The Christian is forgetting that God's grace will be sufficient to meet every future problem or trial. Fear, by its very definition, is an anxiousness or worrisome concern about an "anticipated" future event that might or might not happen. When a Christian is anxious or fearful, he is violating God's Word (cf. Matt. 6:34, 10:31; Phil. 4:6), not perfected in love (1 Jn. 4:18) and failing to trust the sovereignty of God.
    2. He is forgetting that it is through man's weaknesses that God's strength is made perfect. Instead of occupying his thoughts with his own inadequacies, the believer should focus on walking humbly before the Lord so that His power might be revealed at the time of trial.
    b. 1. He experiences the presence of God in a greater way because God draws near to the humble (Ja. 4.8).
    2. He experiences a greater manifestation of the power of God who delights to show Himself strong toward those who trust in Him.
    3. He becomes useful to God as his faith is presented to the world and other Christians as a viable witness. Other answers could apply.

4. They acted craftily by attempting to deceive the people of God.

5. Answers will vary. Answers should include some of the primary attributes of God: righteous, love, holy, mercy, just, good, etc.

6. a. The Gibeonites wanted the Israelites to make a covenant of peace with them.
    b. 1. They disguised their true identity by wearing old clothes and carrying old food in order to pretend they were from a far country (vv. 4, 5).
    2. They appealed to the Israelites' pride by saying that they had heard all the Israelites had done against their enemies and telling them they would be their servants (vv. 8-10). If they had been from a far country, Joshua did not need to make a covenant with them. He could have simply sent them home.
    3. They lied to the Israelites by telling them they were from a far country (vv. 9-13).

7. 1. Ungodly men who will come into churches (savage wolves, Acts 20:29). This is probably a reference to the Judaizers who followed Paul during his missionary travels.

2. Ungodly men who will rise up from within the church and speak perverse things (v. 30, false doctrine and possibly slanderous comments about Paul and the leaders of the church) in order to undermine the ministry and entice believers within the church to follow them.

3. False teachers who masquerade as servants of God (2 Cor. 11:13, 14; 2 Pet. 2:1).

8. 1. They did not remember the command of the Lord or they did not think the command applied in this situation because the Gibeonites told them they lived outside the Land (Ex. 34:12).

2. They answered before they knew all the facts. There appears to have been no pressing reason for the Israelites to have made such a hasty decision. Some further investigation would have revealed the Gibeonites true identity (Pro. 18:13, 17).

3. They did not ask for the counsel of the Lord (Jos. 9:14).

9. The Israelites were not to make any covenants with the heathen nations because they might become a snare to them. This meant that close association with the heathen peoples might cause the nation of Israel to compromise their commitment to the Lord.

10. a. The Christian can have no real fellowship, communion, accord, part or agreement with a non-Christian.

b. 1. A Christian should not marry a non-believer.

2. A believer should not participate in a ministry in which he must work together with non-believers in order to do the Lord's work. Since the things of the Spirit of God are foolishness to the natural (unsaved) man (1 Cor. 2:14), there cannot be a common ministry objective for the dedicated believer and the non-Christian. An unholy alliance of this kind will lead to compromise on the part of the believer in order to promote unity.

3. Other answers could apply.

c. A Christian should make a decision to not marry a non-believer. A Christian should not allow himself to become entangled in business deals and agreements that will cause him to compromise his testimony for Christ. A believer should make a decision to not become involved with Christian ministries in which he will be working together with non-believers for the cause of Christ.

11. a. They grumbled against the leaders.

b. 1. Joshua had sworn by the Lord God and he couldn't violate the covenant with the Gibeonites without bringing reproach on the name or character of the Lord.

2. God would have judged the nation of Israel.

12. 1. They didn't compound their error by violating the covenant they had made before the Lord (v. 18). Two wrongs don't make a right.
    2. They did not react negatively when the people grumbled against them. The leaders had failed and they were mature enough to allow the people to verbalize their disapproval.
    3. They acknowledged their error to the people but also restated their commitment to refrain from violating their covenant (v. 19).
    4. They made the best of their mistake. Instead of allowing the problem to defeat them, they made the mistake work for them (v. 21). God's people can make their mistakes work for them if they learn from them, allow themselves to be drawn closer to God and use them as an opportunity for ministry.

13. Yes. If a believer makes a verbal or written commitment he should fulfill his responsibility. The Christian is instructed to let his yes be "yes" and his no, "no". The believer should not make promises or give an oath. While this perspective might appear to be somewhat idealistic to some, this is the Biblical position for the believer. Realizing he does not live within a society that maintains this type of verbal integrity, the believer should carefully consider what he commits himself to when he enters into an agreement. It would be wise for him to investigate the character of the individual(s) before he enters into an agreement (Christian or non-Christian). He should make sure the contract has a non-performance clause in the contract to protect him if the other party defaults.

14. He should be very certain about the exact details of the agreement. He should make sure there is a provision for his release from his obligations to the agreement if the other party does not fulfill the agreement or there was false information given prior to the actual signing of the agreement. He should avoid all get-rich-quick schemes that do not allow him enough time to carefully evaluate the provisions of the agreement (cf. Pro. 28:22). Other answers could apply.

15. Whether Joshua liked it or not, he had entered into an agreement with some people who had already proved to be deceitful. This violation of honesty would negatively affect any future interaction unless there was reconciliation. Joshua could not violate the covenant, so the only thing he could do was confront the Gibeonites with their deceitfulness and go forward from that point.

16. Answers will vary.

The Final Exam

Every person will eventually stand before God in judgment – the final exam. The Bible says, **"And it is appointed for men to die once, but after this comes judgment"** (Heb. 9:27).

May I ask you a question? *"If you died today, do you know for certain that you would go to heaven?"* I did not ask you if you are religious or if you are a church member; nor did I ask you if you have had some encounter with God - a meaningful, spiritual experience. I did not even ask you if you believe in God, angels, or if you are trying to live a good life. The question I am asking you is this: *"If you died today, do you know for certain that you would go to heaven?"*

When you die, you will stand alone before God in judgment. You will either be saved for all eternity or you will be separated from God for all eternity in what the Bible calls the lake of fire (Ro. 14:12; Rev. 20:11-15). Tragically, many religious people who believe in God are not going to be accepted by Him when they die.

> **"Many will say to Me in that day, `Lord, Lord, have we not prophesied in Your name, cast out demons in Your name, and done many wonders in Your name?' And then I will declare to them, `I never knew you. Depart from Me, you who practice lawlessness!'" (Matt 7:22, 23).**

God loves you and wants you to go to heaven (Jn. 3:16; 2 Pet. 3:9). If you are not sure where you will spend eternity, you are not prepared to meet God. God wants you to know for certain that you will go to heaven.

> **"Behold, now is the accepted time, behold now is the day of salvation." (2 Cor. 6:2).**

The words **"behold"** and **"now"** are repeated because God wants you to know that you can be saved today. You do not need to hear those terrible words, **"Depart from Me..."** Isn't that great news?

Jesus Himself said, **"You must be born again"** (Jn. 3:7). These are not the words of a pastor, a church or a particular denomination. They are the words of Jesus Christ Himself. You <u>must</u> be born again (saved from eternal damnation) before you die; otherwise, it will be too late when you die! You can know for certain today that God will accept you into heaven when you die.

> **"These things I have written to you who believe in the name of the Son of God that you may <u>know</u> that you have eternal life ..." (1 Jn. 5:13).**

The phrase, *"... you may know"* means that you can know for certain before you die that you will go to heaven. To be born again, you must understand and believe (this means to place your faith in) four essential spiritual truths. These truths are right from the Bible so you know you can trust them – they are not some man-made religious traditions. Now let's consider these four essential spiritual truths.

1St Essential Spiritual Truth. <u>The Bible teaches that you are a sinner and separated from God.</u>

No one is righteous in God's eyes, including you. To be righteous means to be totally without any sin, even a single act.

"There is none righteous, no, not one; There is none who understands; There is none who seeks after God. They have all turned aside; They have together become unprofitable. There is none who does good, no, not one." (Ro. 3:10-12).

"for all have sinned and fall short of the glory of God" (Ro. 3:23).

Look at the words God uses to show that all men are sinners – **"none, not one, all turned aside, not even one"**. God is making a point – all men are sinners, including you. No man is good (perfectly without sin) in His sight. The reason is sin.

Have you ever lied, lusted, hated someone, stolen anything or taken God's name in vain, even once? These are all sins. Only one sin makes you a sinner and unrighteous in God's eyes.

Are you willing to admit to God that you are a sinner? If you are, then tell Him right now you have sinned. You can say the words in your heart or out loud - it doesn't matter, but be honest with God. Now check the box if you have just admitted you are a sinner.

❑   *God, I admit I am a sinner in your eyes.*

Now, let's look at the second essential spiritual truth.

2nd Essential Spiritual Truth. <u>The Bible teaches that you cannot save yourself or earn your way to heaven.</u>

Man's sin is a very serious problem in the eyes of God. Your sin separates you from God, both now and for all eternity unless you are born again.

"For the wages of sin is death ..." (Romans 6:23).

"And you He made alive, who were dead in trespasses and sins," (Eph. 2:1).

Wages are a payment that are earned by a person for what he or she has done. Your sin has earned you the wages of death which means separation from God. If you die without ever having been born again, you will be separated from God after death.

You cannot save yourself or purchase your entrance into heaven. The Bible says that man is, *"... not redeemed with corruptible things, like gold or silver ..."* (1 Pet. 1:18). If you owned all the money in the world, you could not buy your entrance into heaven nor can you buy your way into heaven with good works.

"For by grace you are saved through faith and that <u>not of yourselves</u>, it is the gift of God, <u>not of works lest any one should boast</u>" **(Eph. 2:8, 9).**

The Bible says salvation is, *"not of yourselves"*, *"... not of works lest any one should boast."* Salvation from eternal judgment cannot be earned by doing good works – it is a gift of God. There is nothing you can do to purchase your way into heaven because you are already unrighteous in God's eyes.

If you understand you cannot save yourself, then tell God right now that you are a sinner, separated from Him and you cannot save yourself. Check the box below if you have just done that.

❑ *God, I admit that I am separated from You because of my sin. I realize that I cannot save myself.*

Now let's look at the third essential spiritual truth.

3rd Essential Spiritual Truth. <u>The Bible teaches that Jesus Christ died on the cross to pay the complete penalty for your sin and to purchase a place in heaven for you.</u>

Jesus Christ, the sinless Son of God, lived a perfect life, died on the cross and rose from the dead to pay the penalty for your sin and purchase a place in heaven for you. He died on the cross on your behalf, in your place, as your substitute, so you do not have to go to hell. Jesus Christ is the only acceptable substitute for your sin.

"For He (God, the Father) made Him (Jesus) who knew (committed) no sin to be sin for us that, we might become the righteousness of God in Him" (2 Cor. 5:21).

"I (Jesus) am the way, the truth, and the life. No one comes to the Father except through me" (Jn. 14:6).

"Nor is there salvation in any other, for there is no other name under heaven given among men by which we must be saved." (Acts 4:12).

Jesus Christ is your only hope and means of salvation. Because you are a sinner, you cannot pay for your sins, but Jesus paid the penalty for your sins by dying on the cross in your place. Friend, there is salvation in no one else – not angels, not some religious leader, not even your religious good works. No religious act such as baptism, confirmation or joining a church can save you. There is no other way, no other name who can save you. Only Jesus Christ can save you. You must be saved by accepting Jesus Christ's substitutionary sacrifice for your sins or you will be lost forever.

Do you see clearly that Jesus Christ is the only way to God in heaven? If you understand this truth, tell God that you understand and check the box below.

❑ *God, I understand that Jesus Christ died to pay the penalty for my sin. I understand that His death on the cross is the only acceptable sacrifice for my sins.*

4th Essential Spiritual Truth. By faith, you must trust in Jesus Christ alone for eternal life and call upon Him to be your Savior and Lord.

Many religious people admit they have sinned. They believe Jesus Christ died for the sins of the world but they are not saved. Why? Thousands of moral, religious people have never completely placed their faith in Jesus Christ alone for eternal life. They think they must believe in Jesus Christ as a real person and do good works to earn their way to heaven. They are not trusting Jesus Christ alone. To be saved, you must trust in Jesus Christ alone for eternal life. Look what the Bible teaches about trusting Jesus Christ alone for salvation.

> *"that if you confess with your mouth the Lord Jesus and believe in your heart that God has raised Him from the dead, you will be saved. For with the heart man believes unto righteousness, and with the mouth confession is made unto salvation. For there is no distinction between Jew or Greek, for the same Lord over all is rich to all who call upon Him. For whoever calls on the name of the Lord shall be saved (Ro. 10:9, 10, 12, 13).*

Do you see what God is saying? To be saved or born again, you need to trust Jesus Christ alone for eternal life. Jesus Christ paid for your complete salvation. Jesus said, *"It is finished"* (Jn. 19:30). Jesus paid for your salvation completely when He shed His blood on the cross for your sin.

If you believe that God resurrected Jesus Christ (proving God's acceptance of Jesus as a worthy sacrifice for man's sin) and you are willing to confess the Lord Jesus Christ as your Savior and Lord (lord, master of your life), you will be saved.

Friend, right now God is offering you the greatest gift in the world. God wants to give you the gift of eternal life, the gift of His complete forgiveness for all your sins, and the gift of His unconditional acceptance into heaven when you die. Will you accept His free gift now, right where you are?

Are you unsure how to receive the gift of eternal life? Let me help you. Do you remember that I said you needed to understand and accept four essential spiritual truths. First, you admitted you are a sinner. Second, you admitted you were separated from God because of your sin and you could not save yourself. Third, you realized that Jesus Christ was the only way to heaven – no other name could save you.

Now, you must call upon the Lord Jesus Christ once and for all to save your lost soul. Ask Him right now to save you. Just take God at His word – He will not lie to you! This is the kind of simple faith you need to be saved. If you are still uncertain what to do, pray this prayer to God. Remember, the words must come from your heart.

> *God, I am a sinner and deserve to go to hell. Thank you Jesus for dying on the cross for me and for purchasing a place in heaven for me. Please forgive me for all my sins and take me to heaven when I die. I call on you Jesus right now to save me forever. Thank you for saving me now. Amen.*

If you just asked Jesus Christ to save you in the best way you know how, God just saved you. He said in His Holy Word, *"Whoever calls upon the name of the Lord will be saved" (Ro. 10:13)* and the **whoever** includes you – it's that simple. God just gave you the gift of eternal life by faith. You have just been born again according to the Bible.

You will not come into eternal judgment and you will not perish in the lake of fire – you are saved forever! Read this verse over carefully and let it sink into your heart.

> *"Most assuredly, I say to you, he who hears My word and believes in Him who sent Me has everlasting life, and shall not come into judgment, but has passed from death into life." (Jn. 5:24)*

Now let me ask you a couple more questions. According to God's Holy Word (Jn. 5:24), not your feelings, what kind of life did God just give you? _____.
What two words did God say at the beginning of the verse to assure you that He is not lying to you? _____ _____. Are you going to come into judgment - <u>YES or NO?</u> Have you passed from spiritual death into life - <u>YES or NO?</u>

Friend, you have just been born again. You just became a child of God. We would like to help you grow in your new Christian life. We will send you a Spiritual Birth Certificate to remind you of your spiritual birthday and some Bible study materials to help you understand more about the Christian life. To receive these helpful materials free of charge, photocopy the form below, fill it out and send it to us by mail or you can e-mail us at <u>resources @LamplightersUSA.org</u>.

Lamplighters Response Card

❑ I just accepted Jesus Christ as my Savior and Lord on (date) _____,
   200____ at _____.

❑ Please send me the Spiritual Birth Certificate and the Bible Study materials to help me grow as a Christian.

❑ I would like to begin attending a Bible-believing church in the area where I live. Please recommend some Bible-believing churches in the area where I live.

❑ I know of a good Bible-believing church that I will be attending to help me grow as a new Christian.

Name _____

Address _____

City _____ State _____ Zip _____

Email address _____

Lamplighters International, P.O. Box 44725 Eden Prairie, Minnesota 55344